A Husband's Guide to Quilt Appreciation

A Husband's Guide to Quilt Appreciation

John Ryer

Illustrations by Lesley Cox

calico press

A Husband's Guide to Quilt Appreciation
by John Ryer
Illustrations by Lesley Cox

Copyright ©1997 Calico Press, L.L.C.

Originally Published March 1992

ISBN 0-9658286-1-1

Quilt featured as a gift inspired by Four Corners' "Handyman's Dream."

Printed in the United States of America.

For my wife Julie,
who taught me how to appreciate
a quilter and her quilts.

Author's Note

When I married Julie Scott three years ago, I knew that my bride quilted. However, when it came time to move her sewing machine into our new home, I was surprised to learn that there were also boxes of fabric, baskets of unfinished projects, and stacks of quilting books to be moved.

I soon learned that quilting is not a casual hobby: Quilters can be quite passionate about their art. As I learned about quilting, I found myself talking with the husbands of other quilters, sharing with them my thoughts regarding quilt appreciation. I hope this book can expand a husband's understanding of the warmth that quilts and quilters can bring into his life.

I recognize that there are many creative men who work with fabric. In the interest of readability and for the purpose of raising the consciousness of the rest of us, this book is written on the premise that women quilt and men don't understand why.

The Man Who Marries a Quilter...

The man who marries a quilter is a fortunate man indeed. A quilter is rarely a social problem. She is happiest when she is cutting up fabric (perfectly good fabric, as a rule) and sewing it back together again.

This can require a few outings a month to cut up and sew fabric back together again in the company of other women. And then there are those never-ending tours of the world's fabric stores. All in all, she's pretty much a happy camper when she's quilting. A husband could do worse.

The key to proper quilt appreciation is showing interest. If you, the husband, do nothing else, show interest. The least-loved husbandly quilt phrase is, "Gee, honey, that's nice." Next on the loser phrase list is, "But what is it for?"

Quilting is art. **Remember that.** *Art.*

Quilting is a new world to most of us husbands, and most of us plan to keep it that way. However, in the interest of domestic bliss, I recommend a little study into the methods, styles and jargon of quilting.

Quilts and Quilt Blocks

The Quilt Structure:
A Mystery Revealed

Quilts are structured in a similar manner to veneer plywood. The *batting* (that white puffy substance) is the filler. The *backing* can be compared to the lower quality veneer on the backside of plywood. The *quilt top* generally takes the most time to construct. It's the layer with all the colored pieces sewn together.

The *quilting* is the stitching which "glues" the top, batting and backing together into a fabric sandwich.

A *binding* is then added to the edge of the quilt. My wife generally needs encouragement with the binding part — by then she's bored and ready to start another quilt top.

The Quilt Block

Most quilts have a master block which is repeated throughout the quilt. This creates the repetitive patterns which are often seen in a quilt. The master block is usually square but can be any shape. A husband can gain a lot of domestic points by attempting to discern the master block of a quilt. Take a guess; if you are wrong, she will surely correct you.

Quilt Block Types

Many quilt blocks have traditional names. These date back into history — some stir visions of rugged pioneer women conquering the American wilderness.

A *four patch* block is four squares of fabric sewn together. A *nine patch* block is nine squares of fabric sewn together. (Pretty tough so far, huh?)

There are *basket* blocks (hint: looks like a basket), *log cabin* blocks (hint: looks like a log cabin), *bearpaw* blocks (I bet you're catching on pretty quickly to this one) and many others. There is also the legendary *Sunbonnet Sue* block, commemorating her heroic trudge across the great American prairie.

Ask your wife the name of the block that she is using; she will be flattered by your interest.

Crazy Quilts

Don't call the shrink. If she is carrying on about crazy quilts, you need not worry. Crazy quilts are randomly-blocked quilts. They are generally not as safe and reassuring to look at as geometric quilts, but they do fit into the art theme.

Remember to smile and mumble something pleasant when you encounter one of these.

On Point

If you turn a quilt or a quilt block so that it looks like a diamond rather than a square, it is said to be *on point*.

On point is a handy term to carry around in your quilt vocabulary. When confronted with a quilt I often say, "Wouldn't it look better on point?" Sometimes it does, too. Careful, though: if the quilt is already on point you will appear a bit foolish. Of course, foolish isn't always bad, and is better than not showing interest at all.

Hand Stitching vs. Machine Stitching

Quilts that are entirely stitched by hand are *hand-pieced* and then *hand-quilted*.

Quilts that are made using a sewing machine are *machine-pieced* and *machine-quilted*.

Some quilts may be partially hand sewn and partially machine sewn. For example, a quilt might be machine-pieced and hand-quilted.

The Raw Material

It is not uncommon for my wife to embrace a stack of calico and exclaim, "I just *love* fabric." Believe me, she loves fabric, and never seems to have enough of it.

Many quilters use 100% cotton fabric. Apparently synthetic/cotton blends "handle" differently than pure cotton, so to be on the safe side quilters tend to stick to a single medium.

Not being very knowledgeable about quilt fabric, I asked my wife. She said, "The quilters that I know have an uncanny memory for fabric. All those little floral prints might look the same to you men, but quilters are able to detect and remember the subtle differences between the designs. A man who is sent to the fabric store for fabric would do well to take along a generously sized piece of the fabric that his wife wants him to pick up. Then he should seek out a salesperson immediately to help him locate the proper selection."

Apparently my wife has a different idea than I do about what kind of errands a quilt-husband will tolerate. This appreciation stuff only goes so far!

There *are*, however, appropriate times for a husband to venture into a fabric store. But first, take note:

A Fat Quarter is not an Anatomical Part!

There is an interesting term that is used in quilting: the *fat quarter*. The fat quarter is not a result of amassed cellulite. Rather, a fat quarter is a handkerchief-sized square of fabric.

Fabric is usually sold by the running yard. Hint: Visualize Astro-Turf. Fabric stores sell whole, half, quarter and eighth-yard long pieces of fabric. A quarter-yard of fabric is long and skinny, and can be difficult to use. Often a fabric store will cut a half-yard of fabric and then cut the half-yard in two. The resultant quarter-yard pieces are short and fat—hence the name *fat quarter*. Don't mess up on this one.

Become familiar with where the fat quarters are kept at your wife's favorite fabric store. (Knowing the location of your wife's favorite fabric store is not optional.) These squares of fabric make quick and easy gifts that can bail you out during times of domestic crisis. They make great recyclable wrapping paper too!

Fabric & Quilt Periods

Fabric development has followed the many changes of the textile industry. This has resulted in fabric periods defined by fabric types, print patterns and style. Quilters sometimes try to replicate a particular fabric period in a quilt.

It is good form to guess the period that a quilt represents. A quilt which reminds you of that old apron that Grandma used to wear is probably a period quilt. The 1930's is a good first guess.

Touring the World's Fabric Stores

When travelling with your wife, keep an eye out for fabric stores. A new store will delight her, provides a break from driving, and, once again, will build valuable domestic points. It actually is a lot of fun to try to spot

fabric stores as you drive along with your wife. When my wife and I first travelled together, she wanted to stop at every fabric store.

I was patient. Fortunately, patience worked. She slowly became fabric store satiated. (Yes, I know that it is hard to believe.) At that point she got fussy about where she would stop. Since then, visiting fabric stores has become a positive travelling experience.

Waiting

As you may have noticed, you will spend a significant portion of your life waiting in and near fabric stores. Don't fight it—it's part of life with a quilter. You are building up those important domestic points during these waiting periods. A clever husband will recommend stops at fabric stores which are adjacent to sporting good stores and the like. A good fabric store will have a couple of boy chairs near the door, complete with a magazine rack. Pick your waiting turf.

Picking Fabric for Your Wife

Yes, you did read this right. Yes, it is possible.
No, disguise is not necessary.

RULES:

1. Go only to her favorite fabric stores.
2. Ask for help immediately.
3. Look only at fabric intended for quilts.
4. Ask to see the new fabric arrivals—pick from them.
5. Do not choose the colors that you like; rather, pick fabric that reminds you of your wife.
6. As a general rule, stick to 100% cotton fabric.
7. Pick two or three different fabrics.
8. Buy the amount of fabric she usually buys, maybe half or quarter yard pieces.
9. When in doubt, include a gift certificate.

My wife maintains that you get what you pay for: buy only quality fabrics at quality stores. Don't worry, though—if she doesn't like the fabric that you chose for her, she will probably never tell you. (Remember this, girls.) Anyway, she can always trade it with another quilter who has different fabric preferences.

Those Telltale Threads

Don't be embarrassed; a lot of husbands go around covered with threads and small pieces of fabric. This is considered to be the normal plumage for the domestic variety of the *Quilthusband americanus*. In fact, quilting remnants are kind of distinguished looking—right up there with hair from your favorite dog.

No matter how hard she tries, those threads will permeate your lifestyle. Better them than the telltale residue of other vices. Wear them proudly; they are proof that you have made a good matrimonial choice. They can also be a great conversation opener with business associates. Noticing their thread and remnant adornment you might quip, "Say, is your wife a quilter?"

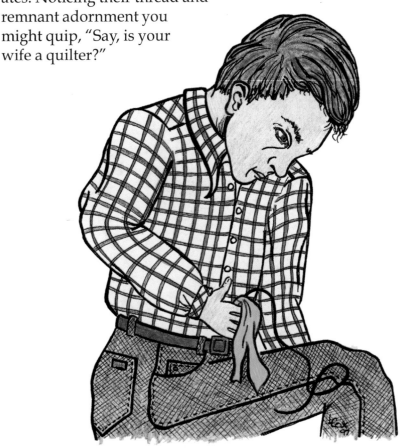

The Quilting Studio

If you ever want to eat at your dining room table again, help her set up a quilting studio. (It may only be a corner of the bedroom, but she'll be happier if you call it her studio.) Her quilting treasures must be stored somewhere. Better in a studio than piled around the rest of the house.

Shelves

Those boxes of fabric that my wife moved into our matrimonial love-nest multiplied with her trips to the fabric stores. She explained that this was her *palette*. It looked like a bunch of old rags to me, but being a sensitive, modern sort of guy I kept my mouth shut and built fabric shelves. My wife was amazed (we were still newlyweds). She said, "I can't believe it; you went out and bought lumber and actually *built me fabric shelves!*" Touching stuff, eh?

The Tools of the Trade

Don't Borrow Her Fabric Scissors
It's hard to make a social problem out of a quilter, but borrowing her scissors is one way to do it. Fabric scissors have to be of top quality and very sharp. If you dull them you'll be in lots of trouble. (Hint to quilters: Leave lots of old scissors in conspicuous spots around the house for borrowing purposes.)

Rulers and Tapes
Quilting being the exacting art that it is, she will have a myriad of measuring devices in her quilt studio. An excellent gift for a quilter is a four-foot long carpenter's ruler — it beats the standard yardstick by twelve whole inches.

These can be obtained from a hardware store.

There is a good chance that she may not know that they exist.

The Cutting Board
Those plastic mats with the lines on them are her cutting boards. (They come in green, white or blue. They are always expensive.) She uses them when cutting fabric. The lines help with measurement and fabric alignment. Cutting boards come in many sizes. There is bound to be a size that she doesn't have that would make a nice present. Ask her.

The Rotary Cutter
She uses that pizza-cutter-looking thing to slice through fabric on the cutting board. Keep your eye on her when she is using the rotary cutter. One slip is all it takes. Shortened fingers can be so embarrassing for a quilter, or for her husband, for that matter.

The Sewing Machine

At last count, my wife had six sewing machines. These are her "old favorite" from her teens, her "new favorite" that does everything but walk the dog, her portable hand-crank machine for camping trips (yes, I am serious—quilting is a way of life around our house), her grandmother's old treadle machine, her serger (which looks like a textile mill but sure trims out trouser legs in a hurry), and a machine from the late 1940's that she says was such a good deal that she Just couldn't resist bringing it home!

If you have less than two sewing machines in your house, consider yourself below average. If she wants a new machine, get involved. Keep her in the discovery and review mode as long as possible. The longer it takes her to pick out a new machine, the longer it will be until she "needs" another.

Seriously though, they do seem to need more than one sewing machine (kind of like having more than one hunting rifle), so don't be surprised when she brings a new one home.

The Quilt Frame

I am told by my wife that I would know what a quilt frame looked like if we had one. (Was this a hint?) Apparently they take up a fair amount of living space. Of course, I am sure that it would be wonderful to have a quilt frame underfoot, along with the six sewing machines and the truckload of fabric. What price love?

Her Great Notions

You will find that there is a multitude of other quilt-related paraphernalia. I generally find them with my bare feet—needles, pins and the like. I also stumble over the associated quilt magazines, stencils, graph paper and so on.

I reserve comment until it all gets over ankle deep in my wife's studio, or becomes a health hazard.

Other Quilters' Husbands

Sooner or later you will find yourself in the company of the husband of another quilter. This can be good.

You may find that you have nothing else in common except that your wives quilt. What to do? In truth, I haven't quite figured this out yet. (I don't think any of us travel.)

Not to worry, though. We quilt-husbands are a noble lot. Our company is often sought after for social functions, probably due to our obvious domestic bliss.

A girl is lucky to have landed the sensitive type of guy who reads this sort of book.

Guilds & Groups

I am told that a woman is happiest if she has at least three separate identities; i.e. mother, wife, and quilter or career, wife, and quilter. With her quilting identity comes involvement with quilt guilds, groups and such.

Think of these groups as positive portions of her quilt identity. My wife belongs to the "Cabin Fever Quilters Guild" and to various subgroups with exciting names such as "Thursday Thimbles" and "Thirteen Easy Piecers."

These groups take up a fair portion of her spare time. My only request to her has been that she spend enough time at home with me so that I remember what she looks like. This has proven to be a successful policy for enhancing our relationship.

Quilts as Gifts

I haven't bought a wedding or baptismal gift since we got married. Not that I'm tight — my wife insists on producing gift quilts for the important people in our lives.

I have taken to underwriting the cost of the fabric for these quilts. This is a no-lose situation where I am supporting her avocation while helping to produce a truly unique gift.

The Husband's Self-Test

How are you doing as a quilter's husband?
Take this quick quiz and find out:

Quiz:

1. Name your wife's favorite fabric store.
2. Name your wife's favorite quilting magazine.
3. Name the block used in your wife's last quilt.
4. Does your wife prefer to hand sew or machine sew her quilts?
5. What are your wife's favorite colors?
6. What colors does she dislike?
7. What is the name of your wife's quilt guild?
8. What is a Fat Quarter?

Handy Quilt Comments

Now that you have enough knowledge to appreciate and discuss your wife's quilts, here are some possible conversation openers:

1. I like your use of color.
2. What a unique choice of fabric!
3. It looks like a quilt from the 1930's.
4. What room will it look best in?
5. Can I hang it at my office?
6. Let's take a picture of you holding it.

Negative Criticism

Approximately one quilt comment in ten should be slightly critical, depending on your wife's tolerance level. This adds to your credibility. If you are like me you won't have to think of any, they will come naturally. For example, I can't stand large floral patterns on fabric. (I am told that these are called "cabbage roses.") So, although I may point out that I like the quilt, I also point out that I don't like the fabric. So far this has worked out quite well.

The Gift List

Give the quilter in your life a gift that she will cherish. Consider one of the following:

New scissors
Cutting board
Rotary cutter
Fabric
Gift certificate (fabric store)
Gift certificate (sewing machine store)
Fabric shelves
Subscription to a quilting magazine
Four-foot carpenter's straight edge
Tuition for a quilt class

And don't forget the most important gift of all —

Your Appreciation!

About the Author

John Ryer was born in Vermont under a 1930's log-cabin quilt. The quilt was one of those non-primary colors that quilters are fond of, and was, appropriately for the era, in the boyish-blue end of the spectrum. John was a hearty lad, daily consuming his ration of cow's milk, love and fresh air, and nightly sleeping under a variety of family quilts.

John moved to Alaska as soon as he figured out where Alaska was. He had many wild and youthful adventures, but kept noticing that his sleeping bag was just a plain solid primary color. While the rip-stop fabric was entertaining, John knew that something was missing.

And so the search for an appropriately available quilter began. This wasn't as easy as it seems as quilter's are a special lot, and not so readily available as one might think from the plethora of fabric stores.

Fortunately, there was one available quilter, Julie Scott, who was looking for an engineer. And fortunately, amidst John's wild and youthful adventures, he had foreseen the need to be an engineer for just such an opportunity.

And so, one sunny August day, John agreed to do all of Julie's engineering for ever and ever, and Julie agreed to do all of Johnny's quilting forever and ever. To this day, Julie has never forced Johnny to sleep under rip-stop. In fact, he has to put on camouflaged clothing, sneak away and go hide out in a tent to do so. Julie is considering inventing the quilted rip-stop sleeping bag.

In addition to writing for Calico Press, John is now a civil engineer working with the State of Alaska Department of Transportation. Julie is self-employed as a retirement planner. They live together in a home that John built, surrounded by quilts that Julie has made, and are delighted that you are reading this book.